Think Rich Grow Rich

The Quranic Way
Hussain Hydrose

Think Rich Grow Rich

About Author 1
Acknowledgment 2
Introduction 3
Chapter 1..7
Chapter 2..10
Chapter 3..17
Chapter 4..23
Chapter 5..29
Chapter 6..35
Chapter 7..42
Section 8 44
Section 9 46
Conclusion 48

1.
2.
3.
4.
5.
6.
7.
8.
9.
10.
11.
12.

Chapter 1

About Author

Hussain Hydrose is a marketing and sales expert with 24 years of experience across various Asian countries. Drawing upon his vast professional background, he has become a renowned speaker and consultant, helping individuals and businesses thrive in a competitive market.

Beyond his corporate achievements, Mohammed embodies the principles of mindful living through an Islamic lens. As a devout Muslim, he believes in integrating faith into daily life, seeking balance and spiritual well-being alongside professional success. His writings and speeches focus on spreading positive vibes, encouraging mindfulness, and promoting inner peace through the teachings of Islam. A passionate traveler, he draws inspiration from his journeys, using them to deepen his understanding of humanity and the beauty of Allah's creation.

Hussain's mission is to help others lead purposeful lives, blending Islamic values with modern-day challenges, and guiding them towards contentment and tranquility in both personal and professional arenas.

Chapter 2

Acknowledgment

ACKNOWELDEMENT ALL PRAISE TO ALMIGHTY ALLAH FOR THE KNOWLEDGE DUAS AND BLESSINGS OF PHROPHET MUHAMMED (SA) AND HIS UMMAH TO MY MOTHER FATHER AND SISTER TO MY BELOVED WIFE AND SON ALL MY WELL WISHERS AND LASTLY MY DEAR READERS FOR THIER PRECIOUS TIME AND WISH ALL SUCCESS IN THEIR ENDEVOUR...AMEEN

Chapter 3

Introduction

Introduction to *Think Rich, Grow Rich – The Quranic Way*

In today's fast-paced world, the concept of wealth and success is often tied to material possessions and financial gain. However, true richness goes beyond bank balances and luxury. *Think Rich, Grow Rich – The Quranic Way* is about understanding that real wealth is not just the money in your hands, but the peace, contentment, and fulfillment in your heart. This book offers a unique perspective, blending timeless Quranic principles with practical tools for achieving success in both your worldly life and your spiritual journey.

What is This Book About?

This book guides you to:

- **Transform your mindset** using the wisdom of the Quran.
- **Balance worldly success with spiritual fulfillment** , ensuring that your pursuits are not only profitable but also purposeful.
- **Cultivate inner peace and gratitude** as a foundation for a prosperous and meaningful life.
- **Understand wealth from an Islamic perspective** , which goes beyond material gains to include spiritual richness, contentment, and contribution to society.

By reflecting on stories from the life of the Prophet Muhammad (PBUH) and his companions, as well as Quranic teachings and Hadith, this book provides actionable steps to help you achieve a holistic form of success. Each chapter offers a blend of spiritual lessons, practical advice, and motivation, designed to help you grow rich both in heart and in wealth.

Highlights of the Book

1. **The Power of Intention (Niyyah)**
Every action starts with intention. This book emphasizes the importance of setting pure intentions (Niyyah) for everything you do, whether it's a personal goal, business venture, or daily activity. When you align your intentions with the purpose of pleasing Allah, success follows naturally.

2. **Trust in Allah's Plan (Tawakkul)**
Effort is essential, but outcomes are ultimately in Allah's hands. This book teaches the balance between making your best effort and trusting that Allah will take care of the rest. By practicing Tawakkul, you'll learn to relieve anxiety and focus on what you can control.

3. **Gratitude as the Key to Abundance (Shukr)**
Gratitude (Shukr) is a cornerstone of the book. It highlights the importance of appreciating what you have as a means to attract more blessings. According to the Quran, the more grateful you are, the more you will receive.

4. **Charity and Giving (Sadaqah)**
Giving to others is not a loss but an investment in both this world and the Hereafter. This book shows how Sadaqah (charity) multiplies wealth and brings peace and joy to both the giver and the receiver.

5. **A Growth Mindset Through Challenges**
Life's challenges are viewed as opportunities for growth. You'll learn to embrace setbacks as part of Allah's plan to help you grow stronger, both personally and spiritually.

Key Takeaways for Daily Practice

1. **Start with the Right Intention:**
   - Every day, begin by setting a pure intention (Niyyah) for your actions. Whether you're going to work, starting a new project, or helping someone, make your intention for the sake of pleasing Allah. This will give your actions greater purpose and ensure spiritual fulfillment.
   - **Practical Tip:** Before you begin any task, take a moment to consciously set an intention. For example, "I am going to work today not just to earn money but to provide for my family and contribute positively to society."

2. **Trust in Allah's Plan (Tawakkul):**
   - While you should always strive for excellence in your efforts, remember that the outcome is in Allah's control. This practice helps reduce stress and fear of failure.
   - **Practical Tip:** After completing a task or making a decision, say "Tawakkaltu 'ala Allah" (I trust in Allah). This will remind you to rely on Him for the results, even if things don't go as planned.

3. **Express Daily Gratitude (Shukr):**
   - Cultivate a habit of gratitude. By appreciating what you have, you attract more blessings into your life.
   - **Practical Tip:** Each night, write down three things you are grateful for, no matter how small. This shifts your mindset towards abundance.

4. **Incorporate Charity into Your Routine:**
   - Regularly give charity, even if it's a small amount. The act of giving not only helps others but also increases your own wealth, spiritually and materially.

- **Practical Tip:** Set aside a small portion of your income (even 1%) for Sadaqah. You can also give in non-monetary ways, such as time, skills, or acts of kindness.

5. **Embrace Challenges as Opportunities:**
   - When you face setbacks, instead of feeling defeated, view them as a means of personal and spiritual growth. Every challenge is a chance to strengthen your character and faith.
   - **Practical Tip:** When a challenge arises, ask yourself, "What can I learn from this?" and make a plan to grow from the experience, trusting that Allah has a purpose for every hardship.

Why This Book Matters Today

In a world where success is often measured by material wealth alone, *Think Rich, Grow Rich – The Quranic Way* offers a refreshing perspective that true richness is found in the combination of spiritual contentment, ethical practices, and material prosperity. It teaches you to:

- **Find balance** between your financial goals and your spiritual values.
- **Achieve more** by aligning your actions with divine wisdom.
- **Live with purpose** , knowing that success is not just about achieving wealth but also about contributing to a greater good.

This book is more than just a guide for financial success—it's a roadmap for holistic growth, helping you achieve true richness in both your worldly and spiritual life.

Chapter 4

Chapter 1

We often find ourselves striving for wealth and success, but what do these concepts truly mean from the perspective of the Quran? Many people equate wealth with material possessions or financial abundance, while success is often measured by societal standards such as career achievements or social status. However, when we delve into the teachings of the Quran, we discover a deeper, more profound understanding of these concepts that transcends the mere accumulation of worldly goods.

In the Quran, wealth and success are regarded not just as ends in themselves, but as means to achieving a **higher purpose** —a life that is pleasing to Allah. This view requires us to shift our mindset and align our goals with divine guidance. It challenges us to see beyond the immediate gratification of worldly gains and to consider the eternal significance of our actions.

The Quran beautifully encapsulates this perspective in **Surah Al-Qasas (28:77), where it is stated: "And seek, through that which Allah has given you, the home of the Hereafter; and [yet], do not forget your share of the world."** This verse provides a balanced approach to life, urging us to strive for success in this world while keeping our eyes firmly set on the eternal rewards of the Afterlife. It reminds us that true prosperity is achieved when we use our resources, abilities, and opportunities in ways that align with Allah's will.

Aligning one's mindset with divine guidance involves more than just acknowledging this principle; it demands an active and engaged effort to integrate this balance into every facet of our lives. It requires that we develop a daily practice of reflection and mindfulness, constantly assessing whether our pursuits and actions are in harmony with Islamic values. When we do this, we begin to understand that wealth is not merely a measure of what we have, but how we use what we have been blessed with. Similarly, success is not just about personal achievements but also about the positive impact we can have on others and our community.

This principle is further emphasized in the Hadith, where **Prophet Muhammad (PBUH) said, "The best of people are those who are most beneficial to people."** – (Al-Mu'jam Al-Awsat). Here, the emphasis shifts from self-centered success to a more communal and altruistic form of achievement. Doing good unto others and being beneficial to society are considered markers of true success. This understanding encourages us to look beyond our individual desires and ambitions and to consider how we can contribute to the well-being and upliftment of those around us.

Moreover, the concept of wealth in Islam extends beyond material riches. It includes the richness of the soul, the wealth of knowledge, the treasure of good deeds, and the abundance of compassion and kindness. By striving to cultivate these forms of wealth, we can achieve a kind of success that is both fulfilling and enduring. This holistic approach ensures that our pursuit of wealth and success is not just about accumulating assets or climbing the social ladder, but about building a legacy of goodness and virtue that benefits not only ourselves but also future generations.

In aligning our mindset with divine guidance, it is essential to recognize the temptations and challenges posed by a materialistic worldview. Modern society often promotes a vision of success that is steeped in consumerism and superficial accolades. To navigate these pressures, we must anchor ourselves in the values and teachings of the Quran, reminding ourselves regularly of the transient nature of worldly goods and the eternal value of spiritual wealth.

One practical way to incorporate this balanced approach into our daily lives is to set intentions that reflect our commitment to both our worldly responsibilities and our spiritual obligations. For instance, when pursuing a career, we can choose professions that allow us to serve and benefit others. In managing our finances, we can prioritize charitable giving and investments that promote social good. In our personal relationships, we can strive to embody virtues such as honesty, generosity, and empathy. By making conscious choices that reflect our dual objectives of excelling in this world and earning the pleasure of Allah in the hereafter, we can create a life that is rich in meaning and purpose. This integrated approach not only brings us closer to true prosperity but also fosters a sense of contentment and peace, knowing that we are living in accordance with divine wisdom.

1. The Business Journey of the Prophet Muhammad (PBUH) with Khadijah

Story: Before prophethood, Prophet Muhammad (PBUH) was a successful merchant known for his honesty and integrity. Khadijah, a wealthy and respected businesswoman in Mecca, hired him to manage her trade caravan to Syria. Prophet Muhammad's excellent business acumen, trustworthiness, and ethical dealings resulted in immense profits for Khadijah, despite the challenges of travel and trade in dangerous and unpredictable desert conditions.

Pain Points:

- Harsh trading conditions: long journeys, risks of robbery, and fluctuating market prices.
- Competing in a marketplace where dishonest practices were common.

Key Takeaways:

- **Integrity builds trust:** Even in competitive and unethical environments, honesty and transparency win long-term success.
- **Hard work and patience:** Despite the tough circumstances of the trading routes, hard work and perseverance paid off.
- **Reputation matters:** Prophet Muhammad's reputation for honesty and integrity led to more business opportunities, including his marriage to Khadijah, which helped expand his influence.

Chapter 5

Chapter 2

Setting Goals with Niyyah

Understanding and implementing goal-setting in the context of Islamic teachings involves recognizing the profound role of Niyyah, or pure intention. Setting goals is not merely about planning for future achievements but also about ensuring that our intentions align with our faith. Islam places significant emphasis on the motives behind every action, thereby transforming even mundane tasks into acts of worship when done with sincere intent. Through the lens of Islamic teachings, goal-setting transcends worldly ambitions and becomes a means of spiritual fulfillment and societal contribution.

In this chapter, we will explore how Niyyah can redefine the way Muslims approach their personal and professional goals. We will delve into the importance of having pure intentions as the foundation of every objective, guided by teachings from the Quran and Hadith. Various practical methods to incorporate Niyyah in goal-setting will be discussed, including self-reflection, articulating goals clearly, breaking them down into manageable steps, and balancing spiritual growth with worldly success. By the end of this chapter, readers will have a comprehensive understanding of how to set meaningful goals that resonate with Islamic values, ultimately leading to a balanced and harmonious life.

Goal-Setting in Islam

Setting goals is an essential component of personal development and success. When approached through the lens of Islamic teachings, it takes on a deeper, more meaningful dimension. The concept of goal-setting within an Islamic framework starts with the notion of Niyyah, or pure intention. In Islam, every action is measured by its underlying intent, making Niyyah a critical element in goal-setting.

Niyyah, as a form of worship, elevates mundane tasks to acts of devotion. By setting goals with pure intentions, a Muslim transforms daily activities into acts of Ibadah (worship), seeking the pleasure of Allah. This approach is rooted in the Hadith, 'Actions are but by intention and each person will have but that which he intended.' This Hadith underscores the importance of having clear, righteous intentions behind every objective we set. It emphasizes that goals should not merely be about worldly gains but should align with one's spiritual growth and the betterment of oneself and others.

The Quranic verse, **'And whatever you spend of good – it will be fully repaid to you, and you will not be wronged.' (Surah Al-Baqarah 2:272)** illustrates the divine support provided to those who engage in righteous efforts. This verse reassures believers that their efforts in doing good, whether in charitable deeds or personal aspirations, are acknowledged and rewarded by Allah. It teaches us that setting virtuous goals with sincere intentions attracts divine blessings and fulfills our purpose as servants of Allah. Hence, the purity of our intentions in goal-setting becomes a key factor in achieving both worldly success and spiritual fulfillment.

Another important teaching is found in the Hadith, **'The best of people are those who benefit others most.' (Sahih Bukhari)** . This Hadith links personal ambitions to communal well-being, suggesting that our goals should not only focus on individual success but also on contributing positively to society. When Muslims set goals that aim to improve the lives of others, they embody the essence of this Hadith. Whether it's through community service, mentorship, or simply being a positive influence, such goals enrich not only the individual but also the wider community. Therefore, goal-setting in Islam encourages the pursuit of personal excellence while fostering collective growth and harmony.

In striving for the Hereafter, we find a harmonious balance between worldly achievements and spiritual growth. Ibn Al-Qayyim, a renowned Islamic scholar, provides profound wisdom on this subject. He suggested that true success lies in seeking the Hereafter, aligning worldly pursuits with spiritual objectives. This alignment ensures that a Muslim's efforts in this world are not in vain but contribute toward ultimate salvation and eternal reward. For instance, an entrepreneur can strive for business success while maintaining ethical practices, ensuring that their wealth benefits their family and community. Similarly, professionals can seek career advancement while upholding integrity and using their skills for the greater good. This dual focus fosters a holistic approach where worldly endeavors complement spiritual aspirations.

To illustrate further, we can look at the comprehensive structure offered by Sûrat Al-Fâtihah, the opening chapter of the Quran. This Surah encapsulates the essence of goal-setting and means-setting. It begins with praise for Allah, acknowledging His sovereignty and mercy. It then transitions into a pledge of devotion and supplication for guidance on the Straight Path. This structure reflects the ideal process of setting goals: recognizing our purpose, committing to righteous actions, and seeking continuous guidance from Allah. By internalizing the teachings of Sûrat Al-Fâtihah, a believer can develop a goal-setting paradigm that balances worldly aims with spiritual commitment.

Furthermore, intentionality plays a pivotal role in goal-setting within the Islamic context. Dr. Muhammad 'Uthmaan Shabeer elaborates on this principle, stating that intentions must be clear and purposeful. Without good intentions, even permissible actions may lack merit. Therefore, when setting goals, Muslims are encouraged to reflect deeply on their purposes, ensuring that their intents are pleasing to Allah and beneficial to humanity. This reflection aligns with the broader principles of fiqh (Islamic jurisprudence), where actions are judged based on their intentions and outcomes. By grounding our goals in sincere intentions, we navigate our lives with clarity and purpose. Overall, goal-setting within an Islamic framework transcends mere ambition. It's about aligning our intentions with the pleasure of Allah, ensuring that our efforts contribute to both personal growth and societal welfare. By incorporating teachings from the Quran and Hadith, Muslims can establish meaningful objectives that resonate with their faith and values. This approach not only enhances personal fulfillment but also nurtures a sense of collective responsibility, ultimately leading to a balanced and harmonious life.

Practical Application of Niyyah in Goal-Setting

Applying Niyyah in daily life is about aligning our intentions (Niyyah) with our actions to create a harmonious and purposeful existence, both spiritually and materially. Understanding Niyyah's role as the underlying intention behind every action and goal is paramount for Muslims striving for holistic well-being.

Niyyah, derived from the Arabic word meaning 'intention,' holds essential significance in Islam. It transforms everyday actions into acts of worship when done with the right intention. The Prophet Muhammad (peace be upon him) emphasized its importance, stating, "Actions are judged by intentions" (Sahih Bukhari). This establishes that having a sincere purpose is crucial, as it defines the value and reward of any deed.

Setting achievable and meaningful goals requires incorporating Niyyah for both worldly and spiritual endeavors. To practically apply Niyyah in goal-setting, begin with self-reflection. Understand your objectives and ensure they align with Islamic values and principles. Ask yourself: Are my goals pleasing to Allah? Will they benefit me in the Hereafter as well as in this world? This reflection helps ensure that your intentions are pure and aligned with your faith.

The next step is to articulate these goals clearly. Write them down and accompany them with a sincere prayer for guidance and success. For instance, if your aim is to excel in your career, make a Niyyah to contribute positively to your community and to use your skills for the betterment of others. This way, your professional aspirations become an act of worship.

Break down your goals into smaller, manageable steps. This approach prevents feeling overwhelmed and allows for consistent progress. Use the SMART criteria—Specific, Measurable, Achievable, Relevant, Time-bound—to define each step, ensuring they are practical and realistic. Incorporate regular self-assessment and accountability to keep track of your progress and to realign your intentions if necessary.

It is also beneficial to integrate spiritual goals alongside your worldly ones. For example, while working towards a promotion at work, set a parallel goal to increase your daily prayers or Quran recitation. These dual objectives foster spiritual growth while achieving material success, creating a balanced life.

The interconnectedness of goals can be beautifully illustrated through the Quranic verse, **"And it is He who created the night and the day, and the sun and the moon; all [heavenly bodies] in an orbit are swimming." – Surah Al-Anbiya (21:33)** . This verse highlights the balance and order in Allah's creation, serving as a metaphor for balancing our personal, professional, and spiritual goals. Just as celestial bodies follow a precise path, our goals should also have direction and purpose, driven by sincere intention.

Balancing professional, personal, and spiritual goals is key to holistic well-being. One practical example is setting designated times for different aspects of life. Allocate specific periods during the day for work, family, and worship. This distribution ensures that no single area is neglected, and all aspects receive due attention.

For instance, a medical professional can schedule time for patient care, family commitments, and individual spiritual activities such as prayer and reflection. By doing so, they fulfill their responsibilities in all spheres of life, fostering a sense of accomplishment and contentment.

Incorporating Niyyah in daily routines can be as simple as beginning tasks with the phrase "Bismillah" (In the name of Allah). This reminder helps maintain the focus on fulfilling actions for Allah's pleasure. Additionally, involving family members in setting collective goals, such as volunteering together or participating in community service, can strengthen familial bonds while serving a greater cause.

It is beneficial to periodically review and reassess your goals and intentions. Life circumstances change, and goals may need adjustment to remain relevant and achievable. Regular introspection ensures that your intentions continue to align with your faith and that your actions consistently reflect those intentions.

Moreover, seeking knowledge and guidance from Islamic teachings can provide clarity and inspiration for setting and achieving goals. Engaging in study circles, attending lectures, and reading scholarly works can enhance understanding and provide practical insights into integrating Niyyah into everyday life.

Balanced living also involves recognizing the inevitable challenges and obstacles. Patience and perseverance are crucial virtues that help navigate difficulties while maintaining sincere intentions. Remembering that Allah rewards efforts based on intentions provides comfort and motivation to persist despite setbacks.

2. Abdul Rahman ibn Awf – The Wealthy Entrepreneur

Story: Abdul Rahman ibn Awf, one of the ten companions promised Paradise, was a successful businessman even before accepting Islam. After the migration to Madinah, he lost all his wealth and had to start over. He was offered financial help by the Ansar (locals in Madinah), but he declined and instead asked to be shown the marketplace. Abdul Rahman worked diligently, bought and sold goods, and soon rebuilt his wealth through honest trading.

Pain Points:

- Losing his entire wealth and resources when he migrated to Madinah.
- Starting from zero in a new environment with no initial capital or contacts.

Key Takeaways:

- **Self-reliance and resilience:** Even in the face of great loss, Abdul Rahman showed resilience and started from scratch, relying on his skills and knowledge.
- **Humility and hard work:** Despite his previous wealth, he didn't depend on handouts and worked hard to rebuild his financial standing.
- **Seek opportunities, not excuses:** Rather than dwelling on his losses, Abdul Rahman proactively sought opportunities in the new marketplace and rebuilt his wealth.

Reference List

Dr Ovamir Anjum. (2022, June 10). *Du"a" As A Goal-Setter* . Al Jumuah Magazine; Al Jumuah Magazine. https://www.aljumuah.com/dua-as-a-goal-setter/

June 2010 – Page 13 – The Quran Blog – Enlighten Yourself . (2010, June 17). The Quran Blog - Enlighten Yourself; The Quran Blog - Enlighten Yourself. https://thequranblog.wordpress.com/2010/06/page/13/

Principles of Fiqh. (2024). *Islam Question & Answer* . Islamqa.info. https://islamqa.info/en/answers/70446/the-difference-between-qasd-objectives-and-niyyah-intention-and-the-importance-of-intention-in-fiqh

The muslim student's guide to university and beyond by idris zahoor . (2021). SlideShare; Slideshare. https://www.slideshare.net/docsforu/the-muslim-students-guide-to-university-and-beyond-by-idris-zahoor-243982159

Chapter 6

Chapter 3

Tawakkul – Trusting Allah's Plan

Tawakkul, the act of placing complete trust in Allah's plan, is a profound cornerstone of the Islamic faith. This concept encourages Muslims to rely wholeheartedly on Allah's wisdom and mercy, believing that He will provide for and protect those who place their confidence in Him. By understanding Tawakkul, one engages in a spiritual journey toward embracing divine guidance and support in all aspects of life. At its core, Tawakkul harmonizes with the belief that human understanding is limited, whereas Allah's knowledge is perfect and all-encompassing. This trust fosters a deep sense of humility and submission, inviting believers to surrender their worries and embrace Allah's grander scheme.

Throughout this chapter, readers will explore the multifaceted nature of Tawakkul, delving into both its spiritual and practical dimensions. The discussion will highlight key Quranic verses and Hadith that emphasize the importance of this principle, offering insights into how unwavering trust in Allah can bring inner peace and resilience during life's challenges. Additionally, examples from Islamic teachings and historical events will illustrate how Tawakkul is not about passive resignation but involves proactive engagement with life's circumstances. Believers are encouraged to make sincere efforts while maintaining faith that Allah's decree is ultimately beneficial. By dissecting these elements, the chapter aims to provide a comprehensive understanding of Tawakkul, underscoring its significance in nurturing contentment, gratitude, and a stronger connection to Allah.

Tawakkul in Islam

Tawakkul, the act of placing complete trust in Allah, is a pivotal concept in Islamic faith. It signifies a profound reliance on God's wisdom and plan, encompassing all facets of a Muslim's life. This unwavering trust underscores the belief that Allah, with His infinite knowledge and mercy, will provide for and protect those who place their confidence in Him.

The term Tawakkul derives from the root word 'wakil,' which means to entrust or assign responsibility. In the context of faith, it translates to surrendering one's worries and concerns to Allah, trusting that He will guide and support. This fundamental principle mandates that Muslims not only have faith in Allah but also act in accordance with His guidance, embodying patience and perseverance regardless of life's challenges.

An integral part of a Muslim's faith and practice, Tawakkul reflects a deep-seated reliance on divine wisdom rather than human intellect alone. It aligns with the perspective that human understanding is limited, whereas Allah's knowledge is perfect and all-encompassing. This acknowledgment encourages believers to adopt a mindset of humility and submission, recognizing that their plans are subordinate to the grander scheme devised by Allah.

The Quran highlights the essence of Tawakkul in several verses, notably in **Surah At-Talaq (65:3): "And whoever relies upon Allah – then He is sufficient for him. Indeed, Allah will accomplish His purpose."** This verse serves as a profound reminder that Allah is the ultimate provider and sustainer. He fulfills His plans in ways often beyond human comprehension, ensuring that those who trust Him are never forsaken.

Understanding Tawakkul involves embracing both its spiritual and practical dimensions. On a spiritual level, it requires cultivating an unshakeable belief in Allah's benevolence and wisdom. Practically, it involves taking appropriate actions while simultaneously leaving the outcome in Allah's hands. This dual approach reinforces the notion that faith without effort is incomplete. Believers are encouraged to strive diligently in their endeavors while maintaining faith that Allah's decree is ultimately beneficial, even if immediate results seem unfavorable.

A key aspect of Tawakkul is the call to remain steadfast during trials and tribulations, confident that Allah's plan is always for the best. Life invariably presents moments of uncertainty and hardship; however, Tawakkul provides a source of inner peace and resilience. This assurance stems from the conviction that Allah, in His infinite wisdom, orchestrates every event with purpose and precision.

Tawakkul also emphasizes that reliance on Allah should not be passive. While it entails trust in divine intervention, it equally advocates for proactive engagement with life's circumstances. This dynamic interplay between action and faith is illustrated repeatedly in Islamic teachings. The believer is urged to make sincere efforts in all undertakings but to rest assured that the final outcome lies within Allah's domain.

Moreover, the principle of Tawakkul fosters a sense of contentment and gratitude. By trusting in Allah's plan, believers learn to appreciate what they have and to accept situations beyond their control. This acceptance nurtures a heart filled with thankfulness, recognizing that every provision and every trial are gifts from Allah designed to enhance spiritual growth.

Lessons from Hadith and Wise Words

Trusting in Allah's plan, or Tawakkul, is a cornerstone of Islamic faith and practice. It requires an unwavering reliance on divine wisdom, a concept deeply rooted in the teachings of the Prophet Muhammad (PBUH) and other scholars. By examining Hadiths and scholarly wisdom, we can gain a deeper understanding of Tawakkul and see how it encourages us to live our lives with patience, perseverance, and a strong connection to Allah.

One profound illustration of Tawakkul comes from a Hadith where the **Prophet Muhammad (PBUH) said, "If you were to rely upon Allah with reliance due to Him, He would provide for you just as He provides for the birds; they go out in the morning with empty stomachs and return full"** (Sunan Ibn Majah)

. This comparison emphasizes that true Tawakkul combines active effort with complete trust in Allah. Birds do not sit idly by waiting for sustenance; instead, they venture out each day, seeking provision while trusting that Allah will provide for their needs. This teaches us that Tawakkul is not about passivity but about making the best efforts in our endeavors while maintaining an undying trust in Allah's plans.

Another source of wisdom on Tawakkul comes from Ibn Ata'illah, who advised, **"Relieve yourself of worry after you have planned, for what Allah has arranged for you is better than what you have chosen for yourself."** This piece of advice underlines that once we have done our part by planning and striving, we should let go of anxiety and trust in Allah's arrangement. This perspective aligns with the essence of Tawakkul, which invites believers to place their hopes and fears into Allah's hands, recognizing that His wisdom surpasses our limited understanding.

These teachings encourage patience and perseverance. The underlying message is clear: human efforts paired with trust in Allah yield the best outcomes. The story of Hajara exemplifies this beautifully. When left alone in the desert with her infant son, she demonstrated Tawakkul by tirelessly running between the mountains of As-Safa and Al-Marwah in search of water. Her unyielding effort, coupled with her deep trust in Allah, led to the miraculous appearance of the Zamzam well. Hajar's story serves as a timeless reminder that Allah rewards earnest striving infused with Tawakkul.

Historical and contemporary examples further reinforce the benefits of Tawakkul. One historical example is that of the early Muslims during the Battle of Badr. Despite being vastly outnumbered and ill-equipped, their unwavering trust in Allah and determined efforts led to a decisive victory. Their Tawakkul did not mean passive resignation but involved strategic planning and courageous action, trusting in Allah's ultimate support.

In modern times, many people find solace and strength in the concept of Tawakkul when facing life's challenges. For instance, someone dealing with a serious illness might relentlessly pursue medical treatment while simultaneously placing their trust in Allah for eventual healing or acceptance of whatever outcome He deems best. This combination of proactive effort and spiritual surrender brings inner peace and resilience, allowing individuals to navigate hardships without falling into despair.

Patience, as emphasized in these teachings, is another critical component of Tawakkul. Patience involves steadfastness in adversity, enduring difficulties with grace, and continuing to strive without losing hope. It is through patience that one can truly embody Tawakkul, recognizing that Allah's timing and wisdom are perfect. The Qur'an frequently mentions the importance of patience, often linking it with trust in Allah. For instance, in Surah Al-Baqarah, verse 153, Allah says, "O you who have believed, seek help through patience and prayer. Indeed, Allah is with the patient."

The act of letting go after exerting one's best effort encapsulates the spirit of Tawakkul. It means accepting that regardless of the outcome, everything happens by Allah's decree and for a reason known best to Him. This acceptance can bring immense peace to the believer's heart, removing the burden of constantly worrying about things beyond one's control.

To illustrate, consider a person striving for a job promotion. They may prepare meticulously, enhance their skills, and perform excellently at work. Despite their best efforts, the promotion may go to someone else. In such a scenario, Tawakkul comes into play. The individual trusts that Allah has a better plan for them, perhaps a more suitable position elsewhere or a different opportunity that aligns better with their capabilities and circumstances. By embracing Tawakkul, they avoid despair and continue to strive with renewed energy and optimism.

Tawakkul also fosters a sense of gratitude, as one learns to appreciate Allah's wisdom in every situation. When one believes that Allah's plans are always in their best interest, even setbacks turn into opportunities for growth and reflection. This gratitude strengthens one's relationship with Allah, leading to a more fulfilling and content life.

3. Uthman ibn Affan – Generosity and Investment in the Community

Story: Uthman ibn Affan was one of the wealthiest companions of the Prophet (PBUH). His wealth was often used to support the Muslim community. When the Muslims of Madinah needed a well for water, the only well available was owned by a man who charged exorbitant prices. Uthman negotiated with the owner to buy half of the well, allowing the Muslims to draw water on alternating days for free. This deal allowed Uthman to earn profits while simultaneously benefiting the community. Later, he bought the entire well and made it free for all.

Pain Points:

- The Muslim community faced a water crisis, and the owner of the well exploited the situation for profit.
- Finding a balance between business and community service.

Key Takeaways:

- **Balance profit with philanthropy:** Uthman demonstrated how wealth can be used for the betterment of the community while still ensuring a profit.
- **Investment with a purpose:** His purchase of the well not only solved a communal problem but also set an example of ethical business practices.
- **Generosity leads to blessings:** Uthman's generosity earned him respect, blessings, and lasting goodwill in the community.

Reference List

أحمد إدريس *IslamOnline* . (2024). IslamOnline; IslamOnline. https://islamonline.net/en/author/idris/

Let Go with the Heart - IslamOnline . (2024, January 31). IslamOnline; IslamOnline. https://islamonline.net/en/let-go-with-the-heart/

Surah Talaq Ayat 3 (65:3 Quran) With Tafsir . (n.d.). My Islam. https://myislam.org/surah-at-talaaq/ayat-3/

Surah At-Talaq - 3 - Quran.com . (2024). Quran.com. https://quran.com/at-talaq/3

Chapter 7

Chapter 4

Auto-Suggestion for Positive Change

Auto-suggestion, a psychological technique rooted in self-induced beliefs and thoughts, serves as a powerful tool for facilitating positive change. When combined with Dhikr, the Islamic practice of remembering Allah, the synergy created can profoundly impact mental and emotional well-being. Dhikr transcends mere repetition, evolving into a meaningful act of spiritual connection that not only calms the mind but also fosters inner peace and contentment. This chapter delves into how integrating auto-suggestion with Dhikr can significantly enhance one's ability to achieve personal transformation and mental tranquility.

In the following pages, we will explore the principles behind auto-suggestion and its effectiveness in promoting positive thinking and behavior changes. We will examine the multifaceted benefits of Dhikr, highlighting its role in reducing stress and anxiety while improving emotional regulation. Through real-life examples and practical applications, the chapter will provide actionable steps for incorporating both practices into daily life. Readers will gain insights into how these combined techniques can lead to a more balanced and spiritually fulfilling existence, ultimately guiding them toward sustained positive change.

Dhikr and Heart Rest

Dhikr, a form of remembrance of Allah, holds immense spiritual significance in Islam. It is not merely a ritualistic recitation but a profound practice that touches the very core of one's being. By engaging in Dhikr, individuals recall and meditate on Allah's names and attributes, fostering a deep connection with their Creator. This act of remembrance transcends any mechanical repetition; it becomes a sincere communication with the divine.

The psychological benefits of Dhikr are vast and well-documented. Research reveals that regularly practicing Dhikr significantly reduces stress and anxiety levels, providing mental solace and clarity. When one engages in Dhikr, it redirects their thoughts from worldly worries to divine remembrance, thereby calming the mind and reducing anxiety. This connection between Dhikr and reduced mental stress can be likened to mindfulness techniques commonly advocated for mental health. As studies have shown, incorporating Dhikr into daily routines can lead to decreased symptoms of depression and anxiety (*The Role of Dhikr (Remembrance of Allah) in Mental Health - Tazkiyah*, 2024). Similar to how mindfulness fosters awareness and presence, Dhikr encourages focus on the present moment while anchoring one's thoughts in spirituality.

The spiritual benefits of Dhikr are equally remarkable. Beyond the psychological relief, Dhikr instills a sense of inner peace and contentment within its practitioners. The regular utterance of sacred phrases or names of Allah nurtures a tranquil heart, bringing a person closer to the divine. This proximity leads to a state of spiritual fulfillment and happiness that material gains cannot offer. **Ibn al-Qayyim elaborates on this by highlighting that the heart contains a void only fillable through genuine remembrance of Allah** (Admin, 2022). This void symbolizes the spiritual need inherent in every human, which, when addressed through Dhikr, results in true contentment.

Consistent practice of Dhikr further strengthens one's faith and connection with Allah. Just as physical exercise strengthens the body, Dhikr fortifies the soul and spirit. Regular engagement in this practice makes the heart softer and more receptive to spiritual truths. A softened heart is more likely to submit to Allah's commands, resulting in greater obedience and alignment with divine will. This submission is the ultimate secret to achieving happiness and contentment, as underscored by **Hasan al-Basri's advice to soften the heart through the remembrance of Allah** (Admin, 2022).

Moreover, Dhikr plays a pivotal role in purifying the soul. The Prophet Muhammad ﷺ stated, **"For everything there is a polish, and the polish of the heart is the**

remembrance of Allah " (Bayhaqī). Just as rust tarnishes metal, heedlessness and sin can corrupt the heart. Dhikr acts as a cleansing agent, polishing the heart and restoring its natural purity. Through consistent practice, individuals can maintain a clean and polished heart, free from the stains of transgression and forgetfulness. This process of purification leads to a more enlightened and spiritually attuned state of being.

Dhikr also enhances emotional regulation, allowing individuals to navigate their feelings with grace and patience. The repetitive nature of Dhikr induces a meditative state, promoting mindfulness and emotional balance. Engaging in this practice helps individuals reflect on Allah's attributes, fostering feelings of gratitude, humility, and reliance on the divine. These qualities, in turn, aid in managing negative emotions such as anger, jealousy, and fear. By regularly reminding oneself of Allah's omnipotence and mercy, one can develop a resilient and composed disposition, better equipped to face life's challenges.

The neurological impacts of Dhikr are no less significant. Engaging in this spiritual practice stimulates brain regions associated with positive emotions and relaxation. This activation leads to a reduction in stress hormone levels and an increase in feelings of serenity and calmness. Scientific studies have corroborated that practices like Dhikr which combine meditation and spiritual reflection, contribute positively to mental health by promoting overall well-being and emotional resilience (*The Role of Dhikr (Remembrance of Allah) in Mental Health - Tazkiyah*, 2024).

Incorporating Dhikr into daily life is not merely about reciting words but about engaging in a meaningful and reflective spiritual exercise. One can integrate Dhikr into various aspects of daily routines—during morning walks, while commuting, or even while performing household chores. This seamless integration ensures that the heart remains constantly engaged in remembrance of Allah, reinforcing spiritual awareness throughout the day.

Hadith on Remembrance

The Hadith **"He who remembers his Lord and he who does not are like the living and the dead" (Sahih Bukhari)** emphasizes the immense importance of remembering Allah. This comparison vividly illustrates the deep spiritual connection that keeps believers spiritually alive through constant remembrance, or Dhikr, while those who neglect it experience a form of spiritual death.

Frequent remembrance of Allah provides numerous transformative effects on one's spiritual life. By continually acknowledging Allah's presence through Dhikr, one cultivates a heightened sense of mindfulness and closeness to the Divine. This practice fosters inner peace and resilience, enabling individuals to navigate life's challenges with greater spiritual strength and clarity. The heart becomes more attuned to the values and ethics of Islam, leading to a more disciplined and morally upright lifestyle. As one engages in Dhikr frequently, this divine connection becomes stronger, enriching their spiritual journey and sustaining their faith even during difficult times.

Incorporating Dhikr into daily routines can be seamlessly woven into various aspects of everyday life. Simple practices, such as repeating phrases like **"SubhanAllah"** (Glory be to Allah), **"Alhamdulillah"** (All praise is due to Allah), and **"Allahu Akbar"** (Allah is the Greatest), can be performed while commuting, doing household chores, or during moments of stillness and reflection. For instance, setting aside specific times during the day dedicated solely to Dhikr can establish a consistent routine that ensures continuous remembrance. Many people find reciting Dhikr after daily prayers particularly beneficial. This not only reinforces the spiritual significance of their prayers but also helps in maintaining a rhythm of regular Dhikr throughout the day.

The contrast between individuals who engage in Dhikr and those who neglect it is stark. Those who consistently remember Allah often exhibit a profound sense of tranquility and contentment. Their lives tend to reflect a balance and harmony, rooted in the reassurance that they are under divine protection and guidance. Such individuals typically display greater patience, empathy, and moral integrity, significantly impacting their personal, social, and spiritual well-being. Conversely, those who neglect Dhikr may experience feelings of emptiness and disconnection. Without this spiritual anchor, they struggle more with stress, anxiety, and despair, finding it challenging to gain the internal peace and solace that Dhikr offers.

Dhikr's role extends beyond individual spirituality; it also fosters a sense of community and shared faith among Muslims. Collective Dhikr sessions, often held in mosques or Islamic centers, provide opportunities for communal worship, strengthening bonds between members of the community. These gatherings serve as a source of mutual encouragement, where believers inspire each other to maintain their spiritual practices and deepen their faith.

Reflecting on the teachings of the aforementioned Hadith, it becomes evident that the continuous act of remembering Allah through Dhikr serves as a lifeline for believers. It animates their souls and sustains them through all circumstances. In practical terms, making Dhikr an integral part of life means using every possible occasion to remember Allah, whether in solitude or among others. By sincerely engaging in Dhikr, individuals not only follow a prophetic tradition but also invite countless blessings and divine peace into their lives.

One illustrative example of incorporating Dhikr into daily life is by beginning the day with morning Adhkar (remembrances). Upon waking up, uttering praises and seeking forgiveness from Allah sets a positive tone for the day. Additionally, as one performs routine activities such as driving or walking, silently repeating short phrases of Dhikr can turn mundane moments into spiritual acts of worship. Over time, these practices can become habitual, effortlessly merging with the ebb and flow of daily life.

Another practical approach is utilizing digital resources, such as Dhikr apps, which offer reminders and guided sessions to help believers stay consistent in their remembrance. These tools can provide structured intervals throughout the day, ensuring regular engagement in Dhikr without overwhelming the individual. By adopting these practices, the reflective teachings of the Hadith are brought to life, enabling believers to experience the profound impact of constant remembrance in their spiritual journey.

4. The Trade Ethics of Sa'd ibn Abi Waqqas

Story: Sa'd ibn Abi Waqqas was a skilled businessman who made considerable wealth during his lifetime. Known for his meticulous honesty, he never compromised his ethics for profit. Once, he was involved in a trade deal where he was offered a higher price for goods due to the buyer's ignorance of the market. Sa'd could have easily taken advantage of the situation, but he chose to inform the buyer of the fair price. Despite losing out on higher profits, Sa'd was content with his honesty and the blessing it brought him.

Pain Points:

- Temptation to take advantage of an uninformed buyer for short-term gains.
- Sacrificing profit for ethical reasons, which could be seen as a financial loss.

Key Takeaways:

- **Ethics over short-term profit:** Honesty in business, even when it costs you in the short term, leads to trust and long-term success.
- **Contentment and trust in Allah:** Sa'd understood that wealth gained through dishonest means would not bring true blessings.
- **Building reputation through transparency:** By choosing ethics over profit, Sa'd earned the trust and loyalty of his customers, ensuring future success.

Reference List

Admin, L. W. A. (2022, September 1). *Dhikr: The Key to Contentment* . Life with Allah. https://lifewithallah.com/articles/dhikr/dhikr-the-key-to-contentment/

Ep: 21: Remembering Allah Excessively | Guidebook to God | Yaqeen Institute for Islamic Research . (2024). Yaqeen Institute for Islamic Research. https://yaqeeninstitute.org/watch/series/ep-21-remembering-allah-excessively-guidebook-to-god

The Role of Dhikr (Remembrance of Allah) in Mental Health - Tazkiyah . (2024, May 11). Tazkiyah - Islamic Personal Development. https://kharchoufa.com/en/the-role-of-dhikr-remembrance-of-allah-in-mental-health/

Chapter 8

Chapter 5

Aligning Thoughts with Quranic Values

Aligning thoughts with Quranic values involves an intentional and reflective approach to life. The principles found within the Quran serve as a comprehensive guide, offering wisdom that can shape our mindset and actions. By internalizing these teachings, individuals can foster a sense of spiritual and moral clarity. This process requires not only understanding Quranic injunctions but also consistently applying them in various aspects of daily life.

In this chapter, we will explore practical steps to incorporate Quranic teachings into our thoughts and behaviors. These include engaging with the Quran through regular reading and contemplation, practicing mindfulness to ensure our decisions align with Islamic values, and seeking communal support to reinforce our commitment. We will delve into specific verses and their applications, providing a roadmap for living a life enriched by Quranic principles. Through self-reflection and accountability, we aim to create a balanced and virtuous lifestyle firmly rooted in the guidance of the Quran.

Integrating Quranic Teachings

Integrating Quranic teachings into daily life is a profound journey that requires conscious effort and dedication. The Quran provides timeless wisdom and guidance, offering a moral compass for personal conduct, character building, and decision-making. Understanding how to integrate these values into our thoughts and actions starts with recognizing their importance and taking deliberate steps to embrace them.

The essence of Surah Al-Fatiha (1:6-7) lies in the plea, **"Guide us to the straight path. The path of those upon whom You have bestowed favor."** This verse encapsulates the central theme of seeking divine guidance to walk the righteous path. It serves as a reminder that aligning oneself with Quranic values begins with a sincere request for God's help and direction. In our daily recitation during prayers, this verse reinforces our commitment to follow the course laid out by Allah.

The Quran is replete with verses that offer clear guidance on personal conduct. For instance, Surah An-Nahl (16:90) states, **"Indeed, Allah orders justice and good conduct and giving to relatives and forbids immorality and bad conduct and oppression."** This verse illustrates the duality of upholding good morals while shunning negative behaviors. To integrate such teachings, one must first internalize these principles. Reflecting on Quranic injunctions and incorporating them into one's mindset creates a foundation for living a life in accordance with Islamic values.

The impact of Quranic values on one's character and decision-making cannot be overstated. When an individual adheres to the principles set forth in the Quran, it shapes their overall demeanor and approach to life's challenges. Practicing patience, as advised in Surah Al-Baqarah (2:153), **"O you who have believed, seek help through patience and prayer. Indeed, Allah is with the patient,"** teaches us to handle adversity with resilience and trust in God. Patience becomes not just a reaction but a cultivated trait that positively influences decisions and interactions.

Moreover, honesty forms a core aspect of one's character as highlighted in Surah At-Tawbah (9:119), **"O you who have believed, fear Allah and be with those who are true."** Embracing truthfulness in all dealings builds integrity and trustworthiness, which are critical for healthy relationships and sound judgment. Therefore, by consistently applying Quranic teachings, individuals develop virtues that guide their choices and behaviors, fostering a balanced and ethical lifestyle.

To fully embrace these teachings, practical steps need to be taken. First, engaging consistently with the Quran is crucial. Regular reading and contemplation of its verses enable a deeper understanding of its messages. Setting aside a specific time each day for Quranic study ensures that these spiritual insights remain at the forefront of one's mind. Another important step is to practice mindfulness in daily activities. By being consciously aware of Quranic values throughout the day, one can make more informed and virtuous decisions. For example, when faced with a dilemma, recalling relevant

Quranic verses can provide clarity and direction. This mindfulness extends to interactions with others, promoting kindness, empathy, and fairness as advocated in Surah An-Nisa (4:36), **"Worship Allah and associate nothing with Him, and to parents do good, and to relatives, orphans, the needy, the near neighbor, the neighbor farther away, the companion at your side, the traveler, and those whom your right hands possess. Indeed, Allah does not like those who are self-deluding and boastful."**

Additionally, surrounding oneself with a community that upholds Quranic values can significantly influence one's ability to adhere to these teachings. Joining study groups or attending lectures can reinforce one's understanding and commitment to living by Quranic principles. This communal support system acts as a motivator and provides accountability.

Implementing Quranic teachings also involves setting personal goals aligned with these values. Whether it's improving honesty, enhancing patience, or increasing charitable acts, having clear objectives allows for measurable progress and continuous growth.

Finally, self-reflection and accountability are essential. Regularly assessing one's actions and intentions against Quranic standards helps identify areas for improvement. Keeping a journal or having a mentor can facilitate this process, ensuring that one remains on the right path.

Applying Hadith and Wise Words

Applying the wisdom of hadith and wise sayings to thoughts and actions is a profound way to align one's daily life with Quranic values. One significant teaching is the idea that kind words are considered an act of charity. As reported in Sahih Bukhari, Prophet Muhammad (PBUH) said, "A good word is charity." This hadith emphasizes that words have power and can be used to foster goodwill, kindness, and a positive environment.

To understand the true impact of this hadith, consider the simple act of offering a compliment or a kind word to someone. Such gestures can uplift spirits, build relationships, and create a more harmonious community. When people use their words thoughtfully and generously, they contribute to a culture of compassion and empathy. The notion that even small acts of verbal kindness are valuable teaches us that our interactions, no matter how minor, can have significant moral weight.

Next, let's analyze Ibn Al-Qayyim's advice on the alignment of thoughts, intentions, actions, habits, and character. According to Ibn Al-Qayyim, "Rectify your thoughts, for they lead to intentions, and intentions lead to actions. Actions, when repeated, form habits, and habits determine character." This powerful statement outlines a clear path from our inner mental states to our outward behaviors.

Thoughts are the seeds of our actions. If one's thoughts are rooted in positivity, faith, and sincerity, it naturally follows that their intentions will align with these values. For instance, if you consistently think about helping others, your intention will be to assist them whenever possible. This intention transforms into actions, such as volunteering or offering support in times of need.

When these actions are repeated, they become habits. A person who regularly engages in helpful behavior will find it becomes second nature to them. Over time, these habits shape one's character, defining who they are as individuals. Thus, by nurturing positive thoughts, we lay the groundwork for developing a virtuous character.

To illustrate the transformative power of integrating such teachings, consider daily interactions at work or home. Imagine a workplace where employees frequently offer each other words of encouragement and appreciation. This practice can significantly improve morale, enhance teamwork, and create a supportive atmosphere. Similarly, within a family, regularly expressing love and gratitude can strengthen bonds and promote a loving environment.

Now, let's discuss practical steps to consistently apply hadith and wise sayings in real-life scenarios:

1. **Mindful Reflection** : Start your day with reflection. Take a few moments each morning to contemplate the kinds of thoughts and words you want to focus on throughout the day. This sets a positive tone and prepares your mind for intentional action.

1. **Daily Reminders** : Use reminders or triggers to keep you focused. For example, set up notifications on your phone with inspirational hadiths or sayings. These reminders serve as a prompt to align your thoughts and actions with Islamic teachings.

2. **Positive Language Practice** : Make a conscious effort to use positive language. Begin by noticing your speech patterns and gently correcting yourself when you speak negatively. Replace complaints with gratitude, criticism with encouragement, and idle talk with meaningful conversations.

3. **Habit Tracking** : Keep a journal to track your efforts. Write down instances where you successfully applied a hadith or wise saying in your interactions. Reflect on how this made you feel and its impact on others. This practice reinforces positive habits and helps you stay committed.

4. **Community Engagement** : Surround yourself with a supportive community. Engage in discussions and activities with like-minded individuals who are also striving to apply these teachings. Sharing experiences and insights can provide motivation and reinforce your commitment.

5. **Learning and Growing** : Continuously seek knowledge. Regularly study hadith and wise sayings, and explore their deeper meanings. Understanding the context and wisdom behind these teachings can enhance your ability to integrate them into your life effectively.

By following these steps, one can gradually align their thoughts and actions with the wisdom found in hadith and the sayings of scholars like Ibn Al-Qayyim. This alignment not only enriches individual character but also fosters a more compassionate and empathetic society.

5. The Prophet's (PBUH) Strategic Business Mind in Treaties

Story: During the Treaty of Hudaybiyyah, the Prophet Muhammad (PBUH) agreed to seemingly unfavorable terms with the Quraysh, including halting the pilgrimage to

Mecca that year. Many companions were disheartened, but the Prophet had a long-term strategic view. The treaty provided a period of peace, which allowed Islam to spread through trade, diplomacy, and personal interactions. Within two years, the Muslim community had grown significantly, and the treaty's terms became irrelevant as the Quraysh breached the agreement, leading to the peaceful conquest of Mecca.

Pain Points:

- Immediate sacrifice of performing pilgrimage and accepting seemingly unfavorable terms.
- Frustration and doubts from followers who didn't fully understand the long-term vision.

Key Takeaways:

- **Strategic patience:** Sometimes short-term sacrifices are necessary for long-term success.
- **Visionary leadership:** The Prophet's ability to foresee long-term benefits from temporary setbacks was crucial to Islam's expansion.
- **Trusting the process:** Even when the situation looks unfavorable, trusting the bigger picture and plan can lead to greater success.

Reference List

Ibn Qayyim – Islam: Message of Peace . (2017). Islam: Message of Peace; Islam: Message of Peace. https://islammessageofpeace.wordpress.com/category/ibn-qayyim/

Pooya, M. M., & Ali, M. A. (2024). *Al-Fatiha (The Opening)* . *The Holy Qur'an - The Final Testament – Juz 1* . https://www.al-islam.org/holy-quran-final-testament-juz-1-mirza-mahdi-pooya-sv-mir-ahmad-ali/al-fatiha-opening

Sun, D. (2019, June). *Reflections on Surah Al-Fatiha* . Daily-Sun; Daily Sun. https://www.daily-sun.com/printversion/details/401086

Words of Wisdom Ibn al-Qayyim . (2020, February 17). Telegram. https://t.me/s/ibnqayyim?before=852

Chapter 9

Chapter 6

Shukr (Gratitude) as a Path to Abundance

Short Story: The Prophet Muhammad (PBUH) always expressed gratitude, no matter the circumstance. Once, he came home to find no food available for dinner. Instead of complaining, he simply thanked Allah and fasted for the night. His ability to remain thankful, even in scarcity, was a key aspect of his character.

Pain Points:

- Facing tough situations such as financial hardship, scarcity, or not achieving what you want.
- The temptation to focus on what is lacking rather than what you have.

Key Takeaway:

- **Gratitude transforms perspective:** Being thankful, even when times are tough, shifts focus from scarcity to abundance.
- **Attracting more blessings:** From an Islamic perspective, showing gratitude opens the door to more provisions. Allah says in the Quran, *"If you are grateful, I will surely increase you [in favor]."* – Surah Ibrahim (14:7)

Key Takeaway in Today's Time:

- **Mental resilience through gratitude:** In today's world of comparison (especially on social media), practicing gratitude helps combat feelings of inadequacy and dissatisfaction.
- **Gratitude as a success multiplier:** Research shows that gratitude boosts mental health and productivity. Start each day by reflecting on things you're thankful for to boost your motivation and attract more opportunities.

Gratitude – The Wealth of the Heart

Gratitude is a powerful principle that shapes our outlook on life. It invites us to appreciate what we have and to develop an attitude of thankfulness. This chapter delves into the concept of gratitude, often called **"shukr"** in Arabic, which holds a significant place in Islamic teachings. The sense of gratitude doesn't rely on the abundance of material wealth but rather it stems from a state of mind and heart. Whether in times of plenty or scarcity, maintaining gratitude can transform our experiences, making them richer and more meaningful.

In this chapter, you will explore the profound impacts of practicing gratitude. The discussion includes the teachings of the Prophet Muhammad (PBUH), who exemplified gratitude in every circumstance, demonstrating how it fosters contentment and resilience. You will also learn about the psychological and spiritual benefits of gratitude, supported by both Islamic principles and scientific research. Additionally, practical steps to cultivate an attitude of gratefulness, such as keeping a gratitude journal and expressing thanks, will be shared. Through these insights, readers are encouraged to shift their focus from what they lack to appreciating the blessings they already possess, fostering a mindset of abundance and well-being.

Shukr (Gratitude) as a Path to Abundance

Gratitude, often referred to as "shukr" in Arabic, is a fundamental principle in Islam that encourages individuals to appreciate the blessings they have, fostering a sense of abundance. A beautiful example of this is seen in the life of the Prophet Muhammad (PBUH). The Prophet always expressed gratitude, regardless of his circumstances. Once, he came home to find no food available for dinner. Instead of complaining, he simply thanked Allah and fasted for the night. His ability to remain thankful, even in scarcity, was a key aspect of his character. This story illustrates that gratitude isn't contingent upon material wealth; rather, it is a state of mind and heart.

Faced with tough situations such as financial hardship or scarcity, many people struggle to maintain a grateful outlook. Financial difficulty can be all-consuming, making it challenging to see beyond immediate struggles. It's common to experience stress, anxiety, and even depression during such times. However, Islam teaches that these moments are opportunities to deepen our reliance on Allah and practice patience and gratitude. By maintaining faith, believers are reminded that everything happens according to divine wisdom and timing. This perspective can transform feelings of inadequacy into contentment, knowing that one's needs will be met in due course.

During tough times, there is a strong temptation to focus on what is lacking rather than what one has. The modern world, driven by consumerism and social comparisons, often exacerbates this tendency. People tend to fixate on their deficiencies, whether it's financial stability, material possessions, or personal achievements. This negative focus can lead to a scarcity mindset, where the individual feels perpetually deprived and dissatisfied. This feeling of lack can create a downward spiral, affecting mental well-being and overall outlook on life.

However, Islam offers guidance to shift this perspective. By focusing on what we have rather than what we lack, we can cultivate a mindset of abundance. Being thankful for even the smallest blessings encourages a sense of contentment and fulfillment. Gratitude is a powerful tool that shifts our focus from scarcity to abundance. When we regularly acknowledge and appreciate the good in our lives, our perception begins to change. We start to see more positives and feel richer, regardless of our financial situation.

The Qur'an and Hadith repeatedly emphasize the importance of gratitude. The Qur'an states, **"And [remember] when your Lord proclaimed, 'If you are grateful, I will surely increase you [in favor]; but if you deny, indeed, My punishment is severe'" (Surah Ibrahim 14:7).** This verse underscores the promise that gratitude leads to increased blessings. By recognizing and appreciating what we have, we invite more goodness into our lives.

Moreover, scientific research supports this Islamic teaching. Studies have shown that practicing gratitude can significantly improve mental health, boost mood, and enhance overall well-being. For instance, keeping a daily gratitude journal, where one writes down things they are thankful for, has been proven to reduce stress and increase happiness. These findings align with the Islamic principle that gratitude opens the door to more blessings and enhances one's quality of life.

In tough times, the temptation to compare ourselves to others who appear more fortunate can be overwhelming. The Prophet Muhammad (PBUH) provided specific guidance on how to manage this tendency. He advised, **"Compare [yourself] to those who are lower than you [in wealth] and do not look at those who are above you [in wealth], for it is more suitable that you do not discount the blessings of Allah"** (*Psychology of Wealth: An Islamic Perspective on Personal Finance* , n.d.). By comparing ourselves with those less fortunate, we can develop a deeper appreciation for our own blessings. This approach helps mitigate feelings of deprivation and reinforces a sense of abundance.

Gratitude also plays a crucial role in navigating financial hardships. It can be easy to fall into despair when facing economic challenges, but gratitude helps maintain a positive outlook. For example, instead of lamenting a loss of income, one might focus on the skills and experiences gained, viewing them as assets that can help rebuild financial stability. This shift in perspective can be empowering, fostering resilience and the motivation to move forward.

In Islamic teachings, wealth is viewed as a test from Allah, but so is poverty. Both conditions require gratitude and humility. The Prophet Muhammad (PBUH) said that for some, wealth may be a greater test than poverty because managing wealth appropriately requires immense responsibility. Believers are encouraged to view their financial status, whether affluent or modest, through the lens of gratitude. Utilizing wealth responsibly and generously reflects an acknowledgment of its temporary nature and divinely ordained purpose.

Charity, or zakat, is another key component tied to gratitude in Islam. Giving to those in need not only fulfills a religious obligation but also fosters empathy and compassion. It serves as a reminder of our shared human experience, breaking down barriers created by economic disparities. Additionally, voluntary charity (sadaqah) further emphasizes the idea that giving does not decrease wealth but rather purifies and multiplies it (*6 Islamic Principles for Achieving Financial Wellbeing* , 2023).

To cultivate gratitude and a sense of abundance, practical steps can be taken. One effective method is to keep a gratitude journal. Each day, write down three things you're thankful for. This simple practice can help shift focus from what's missing to what's present, gradually transforming your outlook. Another practice is to make a habit of verbalizing thanks, both to Allah in prayers and to others in daily interactions. Expressing gratitude aloud reinforces positive feelings and strengthens relationships.

Mental Resilience through Gratitude

In today's fast-paced world, feelings of inadequacy and dissatisfaction are increasingly common, particularly due to the pressures of social media. These platforms often present an idealized version of life, leading many to compare themselves unfavorably to others. Practicing gratitude can serve as a powerful antidote to these negative emotions. By focusing on what we have rather than what we lack, gratitude helps redirect our attention from envy and discontent to appreciation and contentment.

Gratitude, from an Islamic perspective, is profoundly transformative. The Quran emphasizes the spiritual benefits of being thankful. Allah says in **Surah Ibrahim (14:7), "If you are grateful, I will surely increase you [in favor]."** This promise indicates that expressing gratitude not only pleases Allah but also opens the door to more blessings. When we acknowledge and appreciate the favors bestowed upon us, we align ourselves with a divine principle that multiplies those favors. This teaches us that gratitude is not just a passive feeling but an active practice that fosters abundance in our lives.

Scientific research corroborates the practical benefits of gratitude. Numerous studies have found that practicing gratitude can significantly boost mental health and productivity. For example, people who regularly express gratitude experience less stress, anxiety, and depression. They tend to be more optimistic and enjoy higher levels of overall well-being (Komase et al., 2021). This positive mindset translates to better decision-making, enhanced problem-solving skills, and increased productivity at work. The simple act of writing down things you're thankful for can have lasting impacts on your mental health. Engaging in these practices helps create a habit of looking for the good in life, which in turn makes it easier to cope with challenges when they arise.

Reflecting on moments of gratitude also boosts motivation and attracts opportunities. When we acknowledge the positive aspects of our lives, we foster a sense of accomplishment and empowerment. Starting each day by listing things you're grateful for can set a positive tone for the entire day. It primes your mind to seek out and recognize opportunities, fostering an environment where success becomes more attainable. Regularly engaging in this practice makes it easier to recognize patterns of good fortune and know how to replicate them. This reinforcing loop not only enhances personal growth but also contributes to greater resilience against life's inevitable hurdles.

Integrating gratitude into daily routines can take many forms. One effective method is maintaining a gratitude journal where you note down at least three things you are grateful for each day. This practice can shift your focus from what's lacking to what's abundant in your life. Over time, this habit changes your cognitive wiring, making you naturally inclined to notice and appreciate positive experiences. Another useful approach is to express gratitude directly to others. Whether it's a thank-you note, an appreciative gesture, or verbal acknowledgment, expressing gratitude strengthens relationships and fosters a supportive community around you.

Moreover, gratitude does not negate pain or hardship but allows us to see beyond immediate struggles. It provides a balanced outlook where one can acknowledge difficulties and still find reasons to be thankful. Dr. Ashley Smith notes that gratitude acts as a lifeline against negative mental habits that intensify pain. It's about holding both realities—the challenges and the positives—simultaneously (Smith, 2023). For instance, you can be anxious about upcoming changes but still feel grateful for the support system around you. This dual focus prevents overwhelming negativity and promotes a more resilient mindset.

Finally, while the benefits of gratitude are numerous, it's essential to approach it as a sincere practice rather than a superficial exercise. Authentic gratitude involves genuinely recognizing and valuing the gifts and blessings in your life. This depth of recognition can evoke a profound sense of humility and interconnectedness, enriching both your personal and spiritual journey. Although challenges and setbacks are part of human experience, gratitude enables you to face them with grace and optimism, contributing to long-term emotional and mental resilience.

Reference List

6 Islamic Principles for Achieving Financial Wellbeing . (2023, May 22). Zoya Blog. https://blog.zoya.finance/6-islamic-principles-for-achieving-financial-wellbeing/

Komase, Y., Watanabe, K., Hori, D., Nozawa, K., Hidaka, Y., Iida, M., Imamura, K., & Kawakami, N. (2021, January). *Effects of gratitude intervention on mental health and well-being among workers: A systematic review* . Journal of Occupational Health. https://doi.org/10.1002/1348-9585.12290 *Psychology of Wealth: An Islamic Perspective on Personal Finance* . (n.d.). Yaqeen Institute for Islamic Research. https://yaqeeninstitute.org/read/paper/psychology-of-wealth-an-islamic-perspective-on-personal-finance Smith, A. (2023, November 22). *Gratitude - A Mental Health Game Changer* . Adaa.org. https://adaa.org/learn-from-us/from-the-experts/blog-posts/consumer/gratitude-mental-health-game-changer

Chapter 10

Chapter 7

The Power of Charity (Sadaqah)

Subtopic: Giving as a Way to Receive

Short Story: The Prophet Muhammad (PBUH) taught his companions that giving never decreases wealth. Once, Uthman ibn Affan donated 1,000 camels to the Muslim army during a time of great need. Despite giving away so much, Uthman's wealth continued to grow. His charitable actions were not only a source of blessings but also led to immense respect and influence within the community.

Pain Points:

- Fear of losing wealth or resources by giving, especially in times of uncertainty or financial strain.
- Balancing personal needs with the desire to contribute to the community.

Key Takeaway:

- **Charity as an investment:** Sadaqah is not a loss, but a spiritual investment. The Prophet (PBUH) said, *"Charity does not decrease wealth."* (Sahih Muslim)
- **Charity brings blessings:** When you give, you open doors for even more opportunities and provisions, as Allah promises in the Quran: *"Who is it that will lend Allah a goodly loan so that He may multiply it for him many times over?"* – Surah Al-Baqarah (2:245)

Key Takeaway in Today's Time:

- **Corporate social responsibility:** In today's business environment, contributing to social causes can enhance a company's reputation, creating customer loyalty and stronger brand recognition.
- **Giving enhances community and connections:** Philanthropic actions build trust and goodwill, which are valuable in both business and personal networks.

Chapter 11

Section 8

Adopting a Growth Mindset – Quranic Perspective

Subtopic: Embracing Challenges as Opportunities

Short Story: The Prophet Muhammad (PBUH) and his companions faced numerous challenges, including the boycott of the Muslims in Mecca. For three years, they endured hardship, scarcity of food, and social isolation. However, the Prophet (PBUH) saw these difficulties as a test from Allah, an opportunity to strengthen their faith and resilience. This growth mindset helped the Muslims emerge from the boycott stronger and more united.

Pain Points:

- Facing setbacks in business or life and feeling defeated or disillusioned.
- Fear of failure, preventing you from taking risks or pursuing growth opportunities.

Key Takeaway:

- **Challenges are part of growth:** Setbacks are not the end but a necessary part of growth. As Allah says in the Quran, *"Indeed, with hardship comes ease."* – Surah Ash-Sharh (94:6)
- **Embrace failure as a learning experience:** Every challenge is an opportunity to grow and develop, not just in business but in character and faith.

Key Takeaway in Today's Time:

- **Growth mindset in business:** In today's competitive business world, adopting a growth mindset helps entrepreneurs and professionals view challenges as opportunities for innovation and development.

- **Personal resilience:** When facing setbacks like job loss or business failure, understanding that every difficulty has hidden opportunities can help maintain motivation and positivity.

Chapter 12

Section 9

Rizq (Provision) and Wealth in Islam

Subtopic: Understanding and Seeking Rizq (Provision)

Short Story: Once, a companion of the Prophet Muhammad (PBUH), Sa'd ibn Mu'adh, was concerned about his wealth and provision. The Prophet (PBUH) reassured him, saying that Allah provides for His creation, just as He provides for the birds who leave their nests hungry in the morning and return full in the evening. Sa'd realized that while effort is necessary, the ultimate provider is Allah, and worrying excessively about provision is unnecessary.

Pain Points:

- Anxiety over financial security, especially in uncertain economic times.
- Balancing the effort to earn wealth with the understanding that wealth is from Allah.

Key Takeaway:

- **Trust in Allah's provision:** Rizq (provision) is guaranteed by Allah, but it requires effort. The Prophet (PBUH) said, *"If you were to rely upon Allah with reliance due to Him, He would provide for you just as He provides for the birds."* (Sunan Ibn Majah)
- **Avoiding anxiety over wealth:** It's important to make efforts to earn, but stressing over wealth is unnecessary, as provision is already decreed by Allah.

Key Takeaway in Today's Time:

- **Trust the process, but make efforts:** In modern business and personal finance, success comes from striking the right balance between effort and reliance on Allah. Focus on putting in the work without succumbing to anxiety about results.
- **Diversification of income:** From an Islamic perspective, it's important to seek halal income streams. In today's world, entrepreneurs and professionals should focus on diversified investments while trusting Allah for provision.

Chapter 13

Conclusion

Key Lessons from *Think Rich, Grow Rich – The Quranic Way*

1. **The Power of Intention (Niyyah)**
   - **Explanation:** Every action starts with intention, and having a sincere, clear intention ensures that your actions are aligned with divine guidance.
   - **Key Lesson:** Success is deeply tied to your intentions. Ensure that your goals and pursuits are made for the sake of Allah, and they will bring both worldly and spiritual rewards.

2. **Setting Goals with Niyyah**
   - **Explanation:** Setting goals with the right intention is a powerful way to align your aspirations with your faith.
   - **Key Lesson:** When setting goals, focus not just on material success but also on the benefit you can bring to others. This holistic approach leads to greater fulfillment and aligns you with Allah's blessings.

3. **Tawakkul – Trusting Allah's Plan**
   - **Explanation:** While making efforts is important, the outcome is in Allah's hands. Tawakkul (trust) means relying on Allah's plan after doing your part.
   - **Key Lesson:** Trusting in Allah during times of uncertainty brings peace of mind. This balance of effort and trust is crucial for both spiritual growth and financial success.

4. **Auto-Suggestion for Positive Change**

- **Explanation:** Repeating positive affirmations (Dhikr) and focusing on Quranic values can transform your mindset and lead to success.
- **Key Lesson:** Regular Dhikr and Quranic affirmations help maintain a positive outlook, boost mental clarity, and instill confidence, which are essential for overcoming challenges.

5. **Aligning Thoughts with Quranic Values**
    - **Explanation:** Integrating Quranic teachings into your daily decisions helps align your actions with your faith.
    - **Key Lesson:** When your thoughts and actions are guided by Quranic principles (e.g., honesty, integrity), you build a strong foundation for ethical business and personal success.

6. **Gratitude – The Wealth of the Heart**
    - **Explanation:** Practicing Shukr (gratitude) opens doors to more blessings, both material and spiritual.
    - **Key Lesson:** Gratitude shifts your focus from what's missing to what you have, increasing your overall sense of well-being and attracting more positive opportunities into your life.

7. **The Power of Charity (Sadaqah)**
    - **Explanation:** Giving to others through charity is a key to receiving, as Allah promises to multiply the wealth of those who give.
    - **Key Lesson:** Sadaqah doesn't just benefit the receiver; it increases your wealth, fosters community bonds, and attracts divine blessings.

8. **Adopting a Growth Mindset – Quranic Perspective**
    - **Explanation:** Embracing challenges as opportunities for growth is an essential part of both spiritual and personal development.

- o **Key Lesson:** A growth mindset encourages you to see every setback as a stepping stone to greater success. This resilience is not only a personal strength but a Quranic principle.

9. **Rizq (Provision) and Wealth in Islam**
   - o **Explanation:** Rizq is provision from Allah, and while we must strive to earn, we should not worry excessively as Allah has already decreed it.
   - o **Key Lesson:** Make efforts to earn in halal ways, but trust that your provision is already written. Avoid anxiety over wealth, and instead, focus on ethical and purposeful actions.

Overall Takeaway:

This book teaches that success in business and life can be achieved by aligning your actions, intentions, and thoughts with Quranic principles. Through gratitude, charity, trust in Allah, and ethical behavior, you not only attain material prosperity but also inner peace and spiritual fulfillment. Wealth is not just in the physical form but also in the richness of your heart and soul. True growth comes when you view every challenge as an opportunity, act with purpose, and trust that Allah's provision is abundant.

www.ingramcontent.com/pod-product-compliance
Lightning Source LLC
Chambersburg PA
CBHW070419230526
45471CB00006B/2887